BOLDLY I COME

BOLDLY I COME

PRAYING ACCORDING TO GOD'S WORD

KOFI ACHEAMPONG

RISE UP
PUBLICATIONS

Book design by eBook Prep
www.ebookprep.com

Cover design by Justin Stewart
www.justifii.com

June, 2020
ISBN: 978-1-664457-183-5

Rise UP Publications
644 Shrewsbury Commons Ave
Ste 249
Shrewsbury PA 17361
United States of America

www.riseUPpublications.com
Phone: 866-846-5123

CONTENTS

INTRODUCTION

It will be very hard to find in the Bible, or even in the history of the church, anyone God used mightily who did not have a dedicated prayer life. Daniel prayed to God three times a day (Psalm 55:17). The Bible says Jesus often withdrew Himself to go and pray (Luke 5:16). Prayer is a common trait in the lives of the names I have mentioned.

The best quote I have heard about prayer is from Archbishop Duncan Williams. He said, "Prayer is a daily necessity for a daily triumph." When you come to understand that, you will see why prayer is needed by every Christian. Your triumph in life is dependent on your prayer life. I have seen many Christians abused by the devil, all because they don't know the power they have on the inside of them through prayer.

Many Christians desire to pray but don't know how to pray or where to start. Don't feel bad if you are one of these Christians. Even the disciples—who later became the apostles after traveling with Jesus for some time—went to Him and asked Him to teach them how to pray (Luke 11:1-3). If *they* didn't know how to pray, then *you* are in good company. Prayer can be learned. That is why I have put these points together to help you have an effective prayer life.

TWELVE BENEFITS OF PRAYER IN
EVERYDAY LIFE

There are many benefits of prayer in your everyday life. Here are twelve that will encourage you as you use this book to have an effective prayer life.

1. Prayer is an act of humility.

> Then he answered and spake unto me,
>   saying, This is the word of the LORD unto
>   Zerubbabel, saying, Not by might, nor by
>   power, but by my spirit, saith the LORD of
>   hosts.
>
> — ZECHARIAH 4:6

> So then it is not of him that willeth, nor of
>   him that runneth, but of God that
>   sheweth mercy.
>
> — ROMANS 9:16

> I returned, and saw under the sun, that the race is not to the swift, nor the battle to the strong, neither yet bread to the wise, nor yet riches to men of understanding, nor yet favour to men of skill; but time and chance happeneth to them all.
>
> — ECCLESIASTES 9:11

> But he giveth more grace. Wherefore he saith, God resisteth the proud, but giveth grace unto the humble.
>
> — JAMES 4:6

2. Prayer causes heaven to open.

> Now when all the people were baptized, it came to pass, that Jesus also being baptized, and praying, the heaven was opened...
>
> — LUKE 3:21

> Elias was a man subject to like passions as we are, and he prayed earnestly that it might not rain: and it rained not on the earth by the space of three years and six months.
>
> — JAMES 5:17

3. Prayer puts you above nature.

And the Lord spake unto Moses, saying,

Speak unto the children of Israel, that they
turn and encamp before Pihahiroth,
between Migdol and the sea, over against
Baalzephon: before it shall ye encamp by
the sea.

For Pharaoh will say of the children of Israel,
They are entangled in the land, the
wilderness hath shut them in.

And I will harden Pharaoh's heart, that he
shall follow after them; and I will be
honoured upon Pharaoh, and upon all his
host; that the Egyptians may know that I
am the Lord. And they did so.

And it was told the king of Egypt that the
people fled: and the heart of Pharaoh and
of his servants was turned against the
people, and they said, Why have we done
this, that we have let Israel go from
serving us?

And he made ready his chariot, and took his
people with him:

And he took six hundred chosen chariots,
and all the chariots of Egypt, and captains
over every one of them.

And the Lord hardened the heart of Pharaoh
king of Egypt, and he pursued after the
children of Israel: and the children of
Israel went out with an high hand.

But the Egyptians pursued after them, all the
horses and chariots of Pharaoh, and his
horsemen, and his army, and overtook
them encamping by the sea, beside
Pihahiroth, before Baalzephon.

And when Pharaoh drew nigh, the children
of Israel lifted up their eyes, and, behold,
the Egyptians marched after them; and
they were sore afraid: and the children of
Israel cried out unto the Lord.

And they said unto Moses, Because there
were no graves in Egypt, hast thou taken
us away to die in the wilderness?
wherefore hast thou dealt thus with us, to
carry us forth out of Egypt?

Is not this the word that we did tell thee in
Egypt, saying, Let us alone, that we may
serve the Egyptians? For it had been
better for us to serve the Egyptians, than
that we should die in the wilderness.

And Moses said unto the people, Fear ye not,
stand still, and see the salvation of the
Lord, which he will shew to you to day:
for the Egyptians whom ye have seen to
day, ye shall see them again no more for
ever.

The Lord shall fight for you, and ye shall hold
your peace.

And the Lord said unto Moses, Wherefore
criest thou unto me? speak unto the
children of Israel, that they go forward:

But lift thou up thy rod, and stretch out thine
hand over the sea, and divide it: and the
children of Israel shall go on dry ground
through the midst of the sea.

And I, behold, I will harden the hearts of the
Egyptians, and they shall follow them:
and I will get me honour upon Pharaoh,

and upon all his host, upon his chariots,
and upon his horsemen.

And the Egyptians shall know that I am the
Lord, when I have gotten me honour
upon Pharaoh, upon his chariots, and
upon his horsemen.

And the angel of God, which went before the
camp of Israel, removed and went behind
them; and the pillar of the cloud went
from before their face, and stood behind
them:

And it came between the camp of the
Egyptians and the camp of Israel; and it
was a cloud and darkness to them, but it
gave light by night to these: so that the
one came not near the other all the
night.

And Moses stretched out his hand over the
sea; and the Lord caused the sea to go
back by a strong east wind all that night,
and made the sea dry land, and the waters
were divided.

And the children of Israel went into the midst
of the sea upon the dry ground: and the
waters were a wall unto them on their
right hand, and on their left.

And the Egyptians pursued, and went in after
them to the midst of the sea, even all
Pharaoh's horses, his chariots, and his
horsemen.

And it came to pass, that in the morning
watch the Lord looked unto the host of
the Egyptians through the pillar of fire

and of the cloud, and troubled the host of
the Egyptians,

And took off their chariot wheels, that they
drave them heavily: so that the Egyptians
said, Let us flee from the face of Israel; for
the Lord fighteth for them against the
Egyptians.

And the Lord said unto Moses, Stretch out
thine hand over the sea, that the waters
may come again upon the Egyptians,
upon their chariots, and upon their
horsemen.

And Moses stretched forth his hand over the
sea, and the sea returned to his strength
when the morning appeared; and the
Egyptians fled against it; and the Lord
overthrew the Egyptians in the midst of
the sea.

And the waters returned, and covered the
chariots, and the horsemen, and all the
host of Pharaoh that came into the sea
after them; there remained not so much
as one of them.

But the children of Israel walked upon dry
land in the midst of the sea; and the
waters were a wall unto them on their
right hand, and on their left.

Thus the Lord saved Israel that day out of the
hand of the Egyptians; and Israel saw the
Egyptians dead upon the sea shore.

And Israel saw that great work which the
Lord did upon the Egyptians: and the

people feared the Lord, and believed the
Lord, and his servant Moses.

— EXODUS 14

Then spake Joshua to the LORD in the day
 when the LORD delivered up the Amorites
 before the children of Israel, and he said
 in the sight of Israel, Sun, stand thou still
 upon Gibeon; and thou, Moon, in the
 valley of Ajalon.
And the sun stood still, and the moon stayed,
 until the people had avenged themselves
 upon their enemies. Is not this written in
 the book of Jasher? So the sun stood still
 in the midst of heaven, and hasted not to
 go down about a whole day.

— JOSHUA 10:12-13

4. Prayer invites the judgment of God on your enemies.

Hold not thy peace, O God of my praise;
For the mouth of the wicked and the mouth
 of the deceitful are opened against me:
 they have spoken against me with a lying
 tongue.
They compassed me about also with words of
 hatred; and fought against me without a
 cause.
For my love they are my adversaries: but I
 give myself unto prayer.

And they have rewarded me evil for good,
        and hatred for my love.
Set thou a wicked man over him: and let
        Satan stand at his right hand.
When he shall be judged, let him be
        condemned: and let his prayer
        become sin.
Let his days be few; and let another take his
        office.
Let his children be fatherless, and his wife a
        widow.
Let his children be continually vagabonds,
        and beg: let them seek their bread also
        out of their desolate places.
Let the extortioner catch all that he hath; and
        let the strangers spoil his labour.
Let there be none to extend mercy unto him:
        neither let there be any to favour his
        fatherless children.
Let his posterity be cut off; and in the
        generation following let their name be
        blotted out.
Let the iniquity of his fathers be remembered
        with the LORD; and let not the sin of his
        mother be blotted out.
Let them be before the LORD continually, that
        he may cut off the memory of them from
        the earth.
Because that he remembered not to shew
        mercy, but persecuted the poor and needy
        man, that he might even slay the broken
        in heart.
As he loved cursing, so let it come unto him:

as he delighted not in blessing, so let it be far from him.

As he clothed himself with cursing like as with his garment, so let it come into his bowels like water, and like oil into his bones.

Let it be unto him as the garment which covereth him, and for a girdle wherewith he is girded continually.

Let this be the reward of mine adversaries from the LORD, and of them that speak evil against my soul.

But do thou for me, O GOD the Lord, for thy name's sake: because thy mercy is good, deliver thou me.

For I am poor and needy, and my heart is wounded within me.

I am gone like the shadow when it declineth: I am tossed up and down as the locust.

My knees are weak through fasting; and my flesh faileth of fatness.

I became also a reproach unto them: when they looked upon me they shaked their heads.

Help me, O LORD my God: O save me according to thy mercy:

That they may know that this is thy hand; that thou, LORD, hast done it.

Let them curse, but bless thou: when they arise, let them be ashamed; but let thy servant rejoice.

Let mine adversaries be clothed with shame,

and let them cover themselves with their
   own confusion, as with a mantle.
I will greatly praise the LORD with my mouth;
   yea, I will praise him among the
   multitude.
For he shall stand at the right hand of the
   poor, to save him from those that
   condemn his soul.

— PSALM 109

Take hold of shield and buckler, and stand up
   for mine help.

— PSALM 35:2

And Elijah answered and said to the captain
   of fifty, If I be a man of God, then let fire
   come down from heaven, and consume
   thee and thy fifty. And there came down
   fire from heaven, and consumed him and
   his fifty.
Again also he sent unto him another captain
   of fifty with his fifty. And he answered and
   said unto him, O man of God, thus hath
   the king said, Come down quickly.
And Elijah answered and said unto them, If I
   be a man of God, let fire come down from
   heaven, and consume thee and thy fifty.
   And the fire of God came down from
   heaven, and consumed him and his fifty.

— 2 KINGS 1:10-12

5. Prayer changes your story.

> And Jabez was more honourable than his brethren: and his mother called his name Jabez, saying, Because I bare him with sorrow.
> And Jabez called on the God of Israel, saying, Oh that thou wouldest bless me indeed, and enlarge my coast, and that thine hand might be with me, and that thou wouldest keep me from evil, that it may not grieve me! And God granted him that which he requested.

> — I CHRONICLES 4:9-10

> Then said Elkanah her husband to her, Hannah, why weepest thou? and why eatest thou not? and why is thy heart grieved? am not I better to thee than ten sons?

> — I SAMUEL 1:8

6. Prayer prolongs life.

> Then Hezekiah turned his face toward the wall, and prayed unto the LORD,
> And said, Remember now, O LORD, I beseech thee, how I have walked before thee in truth and with a perfect heart, and have done that which is good in thy sight. And Hezekiah wept sore.

> Then came the word of the LORD to Isaiah,
>   saying,
> Go, and say to Hezekiah, Thus saith
>   the LORD, the God of David thy father, I
>   have heard thy prayer, I have seen thy
>   tears: behold, I will add unto thy days
>   fifteen years.

— ISAIAH 38: 2-5

7. Prayer delivers from temptation.

> Watch ye and pray, lest ye enter into
>   temptation. The spirit truly is ready, but
>   the flesh is weak.

— MARK 14:38

8. Prayer brings direction for your life.

> In all thy ways acknowledge him, and he
>   shall direct thy paths.

— PROVERBS 3:6

9. Prayer brings healing.

> And the prayer of faith shall save the sick,
>   and the Lord shall raise him up; and if he
>   have committed sins, they shall be
>   forgiven him.

— JAMES 5:15

10. When we pray, we are doing the work of Jesus.

> And it came to pass about an eight days after these sayings, he took Peter and John and James, and went up into a mountain to pray.
>
> — LUKE **9:28**

> And he withdrew himself into the wilderness, and prayed.
>
> — LUKE **5:16**

> And it came to pass in those days, that he went out into a mountain to pray, and continued all night in prayer to God.
>
> — LUKE **6:12**

> Then were there brought unto him little children, that he should put his hands on them, and pray: and the disciples rebuked them.
> But Jesus said, Suffer little children, and forbid them not, to come unto me: for of such is the kingdom of heaven.
>
> — MATTHEW **19:13-14**

11. Prayer brings us into divine wisdom and insight.

> If any of you lack wisdom, let him ask of God, that giveth to all men liberally, and

upbraideth not; and it shall be
given him.

— JAMES 1:5

Cease not to give thanks for you, making
    mention of you in my prayers;
That the God of our Lord Jesus Christ, the
    Father of glory, may give unto you the
    spirit of wisdom and revelation in the
    knowledge of him:

— EPHESIANS 1:16-17

And it came to pass in those days, that he
    went out into a mountain to pray, and
    continued all night in prayer to God.
And when it was day, he called unto him his
    disciples: and of them he chose twelve,
    whom also he named apostles;
Simon, (whom he also named Peter,) and
    Andrew his brother, James and John,
    Philip and Bartholomew,
Matthew and Thomas, James the son of
    Alphaeus, and Simon called Zelotes,
And Judas the brother of James, and Judas
    Iscariot, which also was the traitor.

— LUKE 6:12-16

12. Prayer changes your appearance.

And it came to pass, when Moses came down
    from mount Sinai with the two tables of

testimony in Moses' hand, when he came down from the mount, that Moses wist not that the skin of his face shone while he talked with him.

— Exodus **34:29**

And as he prayed, the fashion of his countenance was altered, and his raiment was white and glistering.

— Luke **9:29**

HEALING

"who Himself bore our sins in His own body
on the tree, that we, having died to sins,
might live for righteousness— by whose
stripes you were healed."

— I Peter 2:24 NKJV

I wish above all things that you may prosper
and be in health even as your souls
prosper.

— 3 John 1:2

Healing is not only the will of God for His children, it is also a redemptive right. It is the covenant right of every believer to walk in divine health. Not only does God want to heal you, He wants you to walk in divine health. Divine health has already been provided for you through the finished work of Christ. You are not going to be healed; you are healed! The Bible says in John 10:10 that the devil is a thief. The devil wants to steal what belongs to you. You have to take it back aggressively. You have to make up your mind to violently grab hold of what God said is yours. Pray these points with this in your mind: "I am not negotiating for my healing. Whether the devil likes it or not, I am walking in divine health, because Jesus said I am healed."

- Father, I thank You that you are my healer. Begin to praise God that He is your healer.
- Father, I thank You that You are always ready to heal me!
- I thank You that You never turn your back on the sick and You will not turn your back on me.
- Let Your mercy prevail in my life today!
- Forgive me of any sin that may have opened the door of infirmity in my life.
- Let Your power to heal be present in my life today, in Jesus' name.
- Let Your Blood speak for me today!
- I break every curse of sickness in my life by the power of the Blood of Jesus.
- I reject every fear, in the name of Jesus.
- I reject premature death, in Jesus' name.
- I declare I will be satisfied with long life.
- I command every sickness (name your specific problem) to leave my body now, in Jesus' name.
- I release myself from the bondage of sickness, in the name of Jesus.
- I loose myself from any sickness I have genetically inherited from my bloodline.
- I cast every spirit of infirmity out of my house.
- I bind the spirit of cancer, in Jesus' name.
- I cast cancer out of my body, in the name of Jesus.

- I cast out the spirit of deafness.
- I bind and cast out every spirit responsible for this infirmity.
- Lord, let Your power be stirred in me for my healing, in Jesus' name.
- Lord, let every organ in my body function properly and in accordance with Your word.
- Jesus Christ took stripes on His back for my pain, so I ask you, Lord, purge out every trace of pain from my body, in Jesus' name.
- Jesus shed His Blood for my healing, so I ask you, Lord, to purge out all the infirmities, weaknesses, tumors, and toxins in my body, in Jesus' name.
- (Lay your hands on where you're experiencing sickness) Father, as I lay my hands on my body, I receive my healing now, in Jesus' name!
- Father, have compassion and mercy on me.
- Lord, heal me of every hidden disease and infirmity, in the mighty name of Jesus.
- Lord, in spite of every doctor's report, let me receive my healing, in Jesus' name.
- I receive my healing by the precious blood of Jesus.
- I put a demand on the healing anointing of Jesus.
- I receive my healing by faith now, in Jesus' name.
- Lord, release a miracle in my situation!
- Lord Jesus, by Your healing power, I declare I am redeemed from sickness and disease.
- Let the same spirit that raised Christ from the dead quicken me now, in Jesus' name!
- Lord, heal me, and I will be healed!
- I accept the newness of health now, in Jesus' name.

- I walk in good health, in Jesus' name.
- I refuse to bow to this sickness!
- Lord, protect and keep my life.
- Lord, make me whole—spirit, soul, and body.
- Father, repair that which is damaged and replace that which can not be repaired, in Jesus' name.
- Father, satisfy me with a long and healthy life!
- Father, I thank you that I will live my life to the fullest.
- Thank You, Jesus, for my healing!

COMMANDING YOUR DAY

"The steadfast love of the Lord never ceases;
his mercies never come to an end; they
are new every morning; great is your
faithfulness."

— LAMENTATIONS 3:22-23 ESV

"Weeping may endure for a night, But joy
comes in the morning."

— PSALMS 30:5 NKJV

Yesterday's troubles should not determine how today
will be. You are in charge of your today. God has given
you a new lease on life called *today*. Did you know you can
use prayer to determine how your today will be and set your
tomorrow on the right course? The blessings of God are
renewed every morning; everyday is an opportunity to walk
in your divine blessings and to see the manifestation of the
favor of God in your life. No matter how bad yesterday was,

today is a new day. Sorrow may last a night, but joy comes in the morning. This is your morning to be joyful! As you pray these points, you are positioning yourself to receive every blessing God has placed in today.

- Father, I thank You for today. I rejoice in it!
- Thank You, Jesus, for allowing me to see today.
- Father, let Your mercy prevail for me today, in Jesus' name.
- Let every good thing in today come my way, in Jesus' name.
- Father, I commit my day into Your hands.
- Father, I acknowledge You in this day.
- Lord, keep my environment free from evil, in the name of Jesus.
- Father, may Your plan and purpose prevail in life today, in Jesus' name.
- Lord, I commit my going out and my coming in into Your hands today.
- Father, give me strength to overcome every challenge in today.
- Let every evil plan for my life contained in this day, backfire, in Jesus' name.
- Let today be a very fruitful day for me, in Jesus' name!
- Father, lead me not into temptation today.
- Father, grant me a divine escape from all evil today.
- Father, let Your mighty hand be with me to sustain me, in Jesus' name.
- Lord, I receive Your goodness for my well-being today, in Jesus' name.

- I command every blessing to be released into my life today, in Jesus' mighty name!
- Father, may today make a great difference in my life.
- Father, let today bring goodness into my life!
- Father, let my life be a magnet of good things today, in Jesus' name.
- Father, let a miracle be recorded in my life today.
- I declare positive things over my life today, in Jesus' name.
- I declare I shall not fail, but I will excel in all things today, in Jesus' name.
- I declare great doors shall be open unto me today, in Jesus' name.
- I declare great opportunities will come my way today, in Jesus' name.
- I declare I shall not die but I will live to talk about the goodness of God and see the marvelous doings of the Lord.
- I declare that the Lord is good and He has His light to shine upon me.
- I declare by You, oh Lord, I shall run against a troop and I shall leap over every wall.
- I declare the Lord shall equip me with strength and make my way blameless.
- I praise You, God, for the victory You have given me over this day, in Jesus' name.
- Begin to praise God for answering all your prayers (Psalm 118:29).

MARRIAGE STABILITY

"Therefore a man shall leave his father and
   mother and be joined to his wife, and
   they shall become one flesh."

— GENESIS 2:24 NKJV

"Can two walk together, unless they are
   agreed?"

— AMOS 3:3 NKJV

"Two are better than one, Because they have a
   good reward for their labor."

— ECCLESIASTES 4:9 NKJV

A stable marriage is a reflection of God's stable and unfailing love towards His children. Marriage is a reflection or a type, of the marriage between Jesus and His bride which is the church. That is why God is very much interested in seeing your marriage succeed. God wants to use your marriage to show how glorious the marriage between Christ and the church is. If it were up to the devil, there would always be tumult in your marriage but he is a loser. No matter how terrible your marriage has been God will turn it around for you. I see peace coming to your marriage. Your marriage will not end in divorce. As you pray these prayer points, it will undo anything the devil has already done and God will bring restoration in Jesus' name.

- Thank God for how far He has brought your marriage.
- Father, heal every deep wound in my heart that has generated bitterness and hatred towards my wife/husband.
- Lord, help me make things right in my marriage.
- Lord, help me take responsibility for my shortcomings in my marital life and help me work to overcome them, in Jesus' name.
- Father, help us develop good intentions in our marital walk and bring us closer in our union.
- Father, revive the love we once had for each other.
- Father, turn our disunity into unity.
- Lord, let me be willing to recognize and adjust where I might be at fault.
- Lord, give me the wisdom and courage to manage this marriage.
- Father, bring strength to areas where we are weak.
- Lord, give us wisdom to put an end to every misunderstanding.
- Lord, turn the negative trajectory of this marriage to a positive one.

- I come against any impending separation or divorce, in the name of Jesus.
- Father, let our hurt and bitterness be redeemed by healing and love through Christ Jesus.
- I bind every spirit of confusion sent to harass my marriage, in the name of Jesus.
- I rebuke any accusing tongue employed by any household power of wickedness to speak falsehood and curses against me and my marriage, in the name of Jesus.
- Lord, I ask for Your godly counsel to overcome any marital challenges.
- Lord, give me the grace to satisfy my husband/wife according to his/her desires.
- Father, help me offer unconditional love to my husband/wife.
- Let every need of ours be met and keep us on track.
- Father, let us enjoy the fullness of our marriage, covenant, and vows.
- I cast out the spirits creating strife in my marriage, in the name of Jesus.
- Father, let Your perfect will be done in this marriage.
- I come against every third factor (intrusion) hindering the fruitfulness of my marriage, in the name of Jesus Christ.
- Lord, keep each of us from falling into adultery.
- Father, I ask for a productive marital life.
- Let every evil plan against my marriage, be destroyed!
- Let my marital days be enjoyable and honorable unto Your glory, in Jesus name.

- Lord, preserve this marriage, in the name of Jesus.
- I disconnect my marriage from the influence of unfriendly friends, in the name of Jesus.
- Father, do not let us abandon one another.
- I disconnect my marriage from every generational curse of failure on both sides, in Jesus' name.
- Father, let Your grace abide within our marriage.
- Father, let happy days be restored to my marriage!
- I reject every marital disappointment, in the mighty name of Jesus.
- Lord, let peace prevail in this marriage.
- Father, turn the negative in our marriage into positive, in Jesus' name.
- Lord, let any intruder who wishes us evil, be shamed, in Jesus' name.
- Confuse everyone who operates with wrong motives, in the name of Jesus.
- Let our love for each other grow more and more.
- Lord, expose any evil power or person who has been contracted to manipulate my marriage negatively.
- I come against any anti-marriage spirit in the name of Jesus Christ.
- I come against the "fear of divorce", in the name of Jesus.
- I declare my marriage will not break, in Jesus' name.
- Begin to thank God for a blessed and healthy marriage.

WIFE'S PRAYER FOR HUSBAND

"and said, 'For this reason a man shall leave
his father and mother and be joined to his
wife, and the two shall become one
flesh'?"

— MATTHEW 19:5 NKJV

The king's heart is in the hand of the Lord, as
the rivers of water: he turneth it
whithersoever he will.

— PROVERBS 21:1

Marriage is not a competition between spouses. If one spouse fails, the marriage fails. Instead of playing the blame game and trying to change your spouse in your own strength, commit them to prayer!

Pray for the success of your husband. Use these prayer points, asking God to help your husband succeed and be the man of God he was created to be.

- Thank God for your husband and your family.
- Father, thank You for blessing me with my husband.
- Father, thank You for Your favor upon me and my household, because I have found a husband.
- Lord, I thank You that my husband is truly a worthy man.
- Father, I commit my husband into Your hands.
- Father, empower my husband, so that he can take good care of me and the entire household.
- Father, help me to continually love and cherish him as Jesus loves the church.
- Father, please help me to always keep the love I have for my husband and to be faithful and loyal to him.
- Father, bless my husband and let him be satisfied with my love.
- Father, help me satisfy my husband sexually.
- Let my husband only be drawn to me and our family.
- Father, keep my husband focused and help him to always love me.
- Father, deliver my husband from every evil, particular adultery.
- Father, let his love for Jesus Christ be renewed each day as Your love is renewed for us every morning.
- Bless each of us, oh Lord!
- Father, renew and revive our love for each other everyday.
- I neutralize any form of family curse that has followed me into my marriage, in Jesus' name.

- Father, keep my husband strong in You and disconnect him from evil friendships.
- Let my husband be active and productive in all his engagements.
- I bind every demonic power that operates against my husband.
- Father, surround my husband with Your favor and blessing.
- I render powerless any activity of the demonic world against my husband by authority in the name of Jesus Christ.
- Father, let no weapon formed against my husband prosper and let every evil tongue that has raised its voice against him, be silenced.
- Lord, help my husband maintain his masculinity.
- Lord, let my husband obtain mercy and find grace to help him in times of need.
- Father, let your ministering angels always encamp around my husband.
- Father, direct my husband to be responsible in all his ways.
- Lord, let Your peace and glory be with my husband.
- Father, let my husband's days be filled with good health.
- Let the desires of my husband's heart be fulfilled.
- Father, help my husband make Godly decisions by Your Spirit.
- Father, I thank You for answering my prayers.

HUSBAND'S PRAYER FOR WIFE

"and said, 'For this reason a man shall leave
his father and mother and be joined to his
wife, and the two shall become one
flesh'?"

— MATTHEW 19:5 NKJV

The king's heart is in the hand of the Lord, as
the rivers of water: he turneth it
whithersoever he will.

— PROVERBS 21:1

Pray for the success of your wife. Ask God to help your
wife succeed and to be the woman of God she was
created to be. These prayer points will guide you to pray the
right kinds of prayers for your wife.

- Thank God for your wife and your family.
- Father, thank you for blessing me with my wife.

- Father, thank you for Your favor upon me and my household, because I have found a wife.
- Lord, I thank You that my wife is truly a worthy woman.
- Father, I commit my wife into Your hands.
- Father, empower my wife, so that she can take good care of me and the entire household.
- Father, help me to continually love and cherish her as Jesus loves the church.
- Father, please help me to always keep the love I have for my wife and be faithful and loyal to her.
- Father, bless my wife and let her be satisfied with my love.
- Father, help me satisfy my wife sexually.
- Let my wife only be drawn to me and our family.
- Father, keep my wife focused and help her to always love me.
- Father, deliver my wife from every evil, particularly adultery.
- Father, let her love for Jesus Christ be renewed each day as Your love is renewed for us every morning.
- Bless each of us, oh Lord!
- Father, renew and revive our love for each other every day.
- I neutralize any form of family curse that has followed me into my marriage, in Jesus' name.
- Father, keep my wife strong in You and disconnect her from evil friendships.
- Let my wife be active and productive in all her engagements.
- I bind every demonic power that operates against my wife.

- Father, surround my wife with Your favor and blessing.
- I render powerless any activity of the demonic world against my wife by authority of the name of Jesus Christ.
- Father, let no weapon formed against my wife prosper and let every evil tongue that has raised its voice against her, be silenced.
- Lord, help my wife maintain her femininity.
- Lord, let my wife obtain mercy and find grace to help her in times of need.
- Father, let your ministering angels always encamp around my wife.
- Father, direct my wife to be responsible in all her ways.
- Lord, let Your peace and glory be with my wife.
- Father, let my wife's days be filled with good health.
- Let the desires of my wife's heart be fulfilled.
- Father, help my wife to make Godly decisions through Your Spirit.
- Father, I thank You for answering my prayers.

CHILDREN

"Behold, children are a heritage from the
LORD, The fruit of the womb is a reward.
Like arrows in the hand of a warrior, So
are the children of one's youth. Happy is
the man who has his quiver full of them;
They shall not be ashamed, But shall
speak with their enemies in the gate."

— PSALMS 127:3-5 NKJV

You are responsible for how your children turn out. God
has entrusted them into your hands. You are responsible to train them in the way they should go so that when
they grow they will not depart from it (Proverbs 22:6). With
the fast growing technology in this generation and the
corrupted education system, you can never tell what your
children are exposed to. But you can cover them with your
prayers and with the help of God. Susanna Wesley, the
mother of the great John and Charles Wesley, knew divine
intervention was required to raise her eleven children. So she

prayed for them constantly. Today, we are still reading about the things God used her family to accomplish in their generation that has also impacted generations after them. When you immerse your children in daily prayers, the devil will not be able to touch them. Your children will bring you joy not pain, in Jesus name. Your children shall be great, in Jesus' name!

- Lord, I thank You for the child/children You have given me.
- I thank You that You are helping me raise my children.
- Father, in the name of Jesus, I commit my children into Your hands.
- Lord, comfort my children in their time of need.
- Lord, keep my children safe.
- Lord, protect my children against the works of the devil.
- Father, let Your divine plan for my children, be fulfilled.
- Let my children develop strong relationship with You, oh Lord.
- I pray for continual purity and modesty of life for my children, in Jesus' name.
- I pray for healthy relationships with their family, with others, and with You, Lord.
- Lord, keep my children away from the snares of the adversary intended to cut off their life.
- Father, shape their characters and turn their weaknesses into strengths.
- Father, continue to develop their special qualities and abilities for positive influence.
- Let my children be led by the spirit of excellence.

- I blind the eyes of the enemy towards my children with the blood of Jesus.
- Lord, give my children the willpower and the grace to make good choices.
- Father, help my children live a life of godliness and not of wickedness.
- Father, let my children grow in wisdom, favor, and stature like Christ.
- Let every demonic projection against my children be reversed and return back to sender, in Jesus' name.
- Father, help me raise my children based on Your Word.
- Father, let Your righteousness be reflected in my children.
- Father, let my seed remain and let it be prospered.
- Father, let my children seek after Godly things day by day.
- Father, release every spiritual blessing in the heavenly places in Christ Jesus upon my children.
- Lord, let my children be a blessing unto many!
- Lord, let my children increase in wisdom, knowledge, insight, and understanding.
- Father, let my children develop strong self-esteem rooted in their identity in Christ Jesus.
- Father, increase and enlarge the borders of my children.
- Father, let my children be blessed in all they do!
- Father, protect my children from unfriendly friends.

- Lord, establish and preserve the days of my children.
- Father, bless those who bless my children and curse those who curse them.
- Father, let my children be counted among the best.
- Lord, be favorable unto my children!
- Father, be quick to defend my children.
- Father, be quick to fight for my children.
- I declare my children will never fail, in Jesus' name.
- I declare favor, honor, success, and increase upon my children.
- Lord, I worship and praise Your name for all my children.
- Lord, thank You for answering all my prayers.

FRUIT OF THE WOMB

"No one shall suffer miscarriage or be barren
in your land; I will fulfill the number of
your days."

— Exodus **23:26 NKJV**

The first task God gave to mankind is "be fruitful and multiply" (Genesis 1:28). God loves children and wants you to have children. Barrenness is not your portion. Not only will you have as many children as you desire, your children are going to be a blessing (Psalm 37:26).

I see you carrying your own child a year from today.

- Father, I thank You for Your faithfulness.
- I thank You that You are a merciful God.
- Father, let Your mercy prevail for me today, in Jesus' name.
- I plead the blood of Jesus to grant me audience before the throne of grace.
- Father, help me in this childless state.

- Faithful God, remember Your covenant concerning child-bearing and act quickly to perfect all that concerns me.
- I break every demonic blockage against the fruitfulness of my womb, in Jesus' name.
- I break the control of any self-imposed curse which has affected the fruitfulness of my womb.
- I root out any household curse of barrenness issued against my family line.
- I disconnect myself from any ancestral and parental evil covenant of barrenness that may have been unconsciously established in my family, in the name of Jesus.
- Lord, roll away any reproach of barrenness from my life.
- Father, show me mercy as You did for Hannah and give me a child!
- Father, I call upon You in this time of great need; bless me with my own child, in Jesus' name.
- I invoke the power of God to run through me to put to order any defective organ, cell, or tissue.
- Father, let my reproductive system be active and productive.
- Let my womb begin to produce fruit.
- Father, I ask for divine and total restoration of my reproductive system.
- Oh Lord, my trust is fully in You! Do not let my expectation be cut off!
- Father, take away every mark of unfruitfulness from my life.
- Lord, give me the gift of motherhood/fatherhood.
- Lord, deliver me from barrenness.
- Let me be a mother/father of many.

- Father, override every medical report and give me a miracle!
- Father, replace my sorrows and pain with joy and gladness!
- Lord, hear my desperate cry and let me be called a mother/father!
- Father, do not let me remain childless.
- Father, have pity on me and harken to my desperate prayers!
- Father, uncover every demonic covering on my womb and make it possible for me to carry and bear children.
- Lord, make my reproductive system fertile.
- Bless me with children and an everlasting lineage.
- Let those who laugh at me, bow their heads in shame.
- Let me see my children's children!
- Let every dead organ in my body, be activated for fertility, in Jesus' name.
- Oh God, let this season be the season of Your manifestations.
- Let there be a performance of Your word in my life.
- Let there be a great "spark" in every encounter I have with my partner after this prayer.
- Father, let me bring forth powerful seeds.
- Make my children exceedingly great.
- I thank You, Lord, for answered prayers.
- I sing praises unto You for al You have done.

ALSO FROM REVIVAL TODAY

Dominion Over Sickness and Disease

Boldly I Come

ABOUT THE AUTHOR

Evangelist Kofi Acheampong and his wife ChiChi co-founded World Evangelistic Ministries in 2016. They share a mission to preach the Gospel, win souls, and empower Christians to operate in the gifts of the Holy Spirit.

Ev. Kofi travels extensively with the ministry of Evangelist Jonathan Shuttlesworth, co-founder of Revival Today, and faithfully leads the vital Prayer Ministry.

To learn more about the ministry of Revival Today or World Evangelistic Ministries, please visit the following websites:

WWW.REVIVALTODAY.COM
WWW.WORLDEVANGELISTIC.COM

Connect with Evangelist Kofi Acheampong:

facebook.com/worldevangelistic

twitter.com/evangelistkofia

instagram.com/evangelist_kofi

youtube.com/RevivalToday07

Printed in the USA
CPSIA information can be obtained
at www.ICGtesting.com
LVHW040427130824
788023LV00012B/785